PRESSED BUT NOT CRUSHED

Pressed But Not Crushed - 30 Day Devotional Journal
Copyright © 2024 by Cassandra Bellevue

Published by: Bellevue Production Co.
www.CassandraBellevue.com

All rights reserved. No part of this publication may be reproduced, stored in or introduced into a retrieval system, or transmitted, in any form, or by any means (electronic, mechanical, photocopying, recording, or otherwise), without the prior permission of the publisher.

ISBN: 978-1-7358277-4-2 (Paperback)

Scriptures marked NLT are taken from the Holy Bible, New Living Translation, copyright © 1996, 2004, 2015 by Tyndale House Foundation. Used by permission of Tyndale House Publishers, a Division of Tyndale House Ministries, Carol Stream, Illinois 60188. All rights reserved.

Scriptures marked NKJV are taken from the New King James Version®. Copyright © 1982 by Thomas Nelson. Used by permission. All rights reserved. Scriptures marked KJV are taken from the KING JAMES VERSION (KJV): KING JAMES VERSION, public domain.

Scripture quotations marked TPT are from The Passion Translation®. Copyright © 2017, 2018, 2020 by Passion & Fire Ministries, Inc. Used by permission. All rights reserved. ThePassionTranslation.com.

2nd edition.
Printed and bound in the United States of America.

CONTENTS

Introduction	1
WEEK 1	3
WEEK 2	18
WEEK 3	34
WEEK 4	50
WEEK 5	66
WEEK 6	84
Review and Celebrate	99
Final Declaration and Prayer	103

Introduction

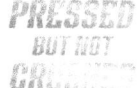

Welcome to the *Pressed But Not Crushed Companion Guide*. Surprise! Surprise! No one was more shocked than I was when so many of you who read *Pressed But Not Crushed* requested that I write a follow-up Bible study! The testimonies I received via DMs, text messages, and phone calls left me in awe of how the Lord was touching so many hearts. I'm so grateful for those of you who are going hard after your healing and purpose. I sense the hunger and determination to partner with God on your calling and destiny.

This six-week study, or companion guide, is just another avenue to dive deeper into the material and gain more revelation. This is just one more way to press into God for more strategy and get completely free from all those things that try to hinder. This devotional is written to facilitate a deeper dive, whether it's individually or with a group.

You have two options, well actually three, on how to navigate through this companion guide. For my friends who like to do their devotionals Monday thru Friday, this will be a six-week study guide with five daily sessions each week. For my friends who like to power through the weekends as well, this will be a 30-day study guide. The third option? Well, that one is for my less structured friends who just want to take their time and go at their own pace. There's grace for that as well. However you decide to partake, come with your heart positioned and ready to encounter your heavenly Father.

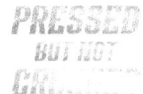

If you haven't had a chance to jump into the book yet, we unpack the Armor of God presented in Ephesians. In this companion guide, we will focus on one piece of armor every week for those doing the six-week track. Are you as excited as I am? The main prayer I have prayed over this book, and every person who reads it, is that God would meet you exactly where you are and speak to you very clearly. After hearing so many testimonials, my faith has increased to believe He will do that and more for you throughout this devotional.

As we sojourn together, there is one very important truth that we need to get on the same page concerning. You can hear God's voice. YES, YOU! John 10:17 (TPT) says, "My own sheep will hear my voice and I know each one, and they will follow me." God wants to talk to you personally. We'll be inviting Him to speak to you throughout this devotional. These intimate times will be called ***activations***. When you see the word "Activation" on the page, that's your cue to pray, "Holy Spirit, come clear the airways so I can hear Your voice clearly without interference." We're going to work out your spiritual listening muscle and it's going to be GREAT!

Thank you for giving me the honor to spend even more time with you in this season. Your time is precious to me. May you find this to be a life-changing journey that was worth every minute of your time, commitment, and sacrifice.

The Best is Yet to Come!
Cassandra Bellevue

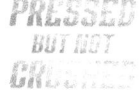

WEEK 1

Chapters 1 – 5

During week one, we will cover chapters 1 – 5 from the book *Pressed But Not Crushed*. This includes the introduction chapters and our first piece of armor, The Belt of Truth. No need to panic! During weeks 2 – 5, we'll only cover two chapters a week (or every five days.) And during week 6 we'll cover the last four chapters of the book.

As we launch, I want you to ask *yourself* the following questions:

What am I looking to get out of this study?

_____
_____
_____
_____
_____
_____
_____
_____

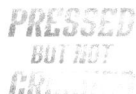

What piece of armor am I most looking forward to discussing and why?

_____
_____
_____
_____
_____
_____

Now I want you to ask *Holy Spirit* the next question:

Which piece of armor needs to be strengthened the *most* in my life?

_____
_____
_____
_____
_____

At the end on this study, we'll come back to these questions and see how far we've come.

Are you ready? Let's get to it!

Week 1: Day 1

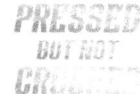

When you first saw the title of the book and the cover, what thoughts came to mind?

_____
_____
_____
_____
_____

On the surface, what does the phrase "Pressed, But Not Crushed" mean to you?

_____
_____
_____
_____
_____

Second Corinthians 4:8 NLT says, "We are pressed on every side by troubles, but we are not crushed. We are perplexed but not driven to despair."

What feelings does that scripture bring to the surface?

_____
_____
_____
_____
_____

Does this scripture change your initial interpretation of the book's title? If so, how?

_____
_____
_____
_____
_____

Why do you feel that you were drawn to this book/study?

_____
_____
_____
_____
_____

There are many lessons and encouragements I hope each person walks away with after reading the book and doing this devotional. However, the number one sentiment I hope you take away from this experience is that … with God you are undefeatable.

When I talk to my life coaching clients, I am constantly stressing to them this one truth. No matter what they are going through, whatever it is that's pressing them in life, it will not succeed. It will not crush/defeat them as long as Jesus Christ is at the center of their walk and they lean into Him during the process.

But first we must establish trust! We must be convinced, without a shadow of a doubt, that He sees us, loves us, and is for us. The Bible tells us that God knew us and knit us in our mother's womb (Psalm 139:13)! So, does He see you? Yes. But are you convinced He loves you and is for you?

If you haven't gotten to Chapter 5 yet, spoiler alert, you will find my personal salvation testimony there. Everyone's journey to destiny kicks into a higher gear once they receive Jesus Christ as their personal Lord and Savior.

What is your story? How did that pivotal moment play out in your life?

_____
_____
_____
_____
_____
_____
_____
_____
_____
_____
_____
_____
_____

"Giving my life to Christ is single-handedly the best decision I've ever made in my entire life."

ACTIVATION

Or have you yet to give Him your *yes*? If you haven't, I want you to ask Him:

"Jesus, what is holding me back from surrendering my life into Your loving, capable hands?"

_____
_____
_____
_____
_____
_____

Whatever He shows you, continue the conversation until you feel His peace. Then when you're ready, pray:

Jesus, I repent for living my life on my own term and for all the sin and mistakes I participated in along the way. Thank You for Your sacrifice that is the bridge to reconcile me back to the Father. I surrender my life to You and ask You to be Lord of my life today and forever.

Week 1: Day 2

I'm a firm believer that God will use anything to speak to us to get our attention. Remember Jonah and the big fish? Remember the donkey talking in Numbers 22:28? I encourage you to read those stories if you haven't before. You'll never forget it.

It's so important to give Holy Spirit room to speak to us the way He wants to, using whatever method He chooses. I shared in chapter 2 of *Pressed But Not Crushed* how Holy Spirit redirected my plans one evening in order to set up a personal encounter for me… at a movie theater no less!

He used the themes within the movies to touch a very tender place in my heart and minister healing.

Do you find yourself surprised by that? Which of the following explains your answer best?

A. I have a hard time believing God speaks to us personally.
B. I've never experienced Him speaking to me in such a personal way.
C. It's happened once or twice but certainly not the norm.
D. I experience Him speaking to me on a regular/daily basis.

Whatever your answer is, just know that God wants you experiencing Him speaking to you … every single day. He wants to meet with you, converse with you, and strengthen His

"If you don't know God, get to know Him… He caters to us individually. How you experience God will be unique to you and the very best part of your life"

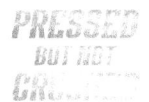

personal relationship with you. That's what the Christian walk is supposed to be: a personal relationship.

So now that we know God wants to speak to us on a regular basis, how will you make room for that to happen going forward?

Ask Holy Spirit…. **"What steps can I take, starting today, to experience You in a more personal way?"**

_____
_____
_____
_____
_____
_____
_____
_____
_____
_____

ACTIVATION

Week 1: Day 3

I love to see people growing and maturing. No matter how small the win is, we want to celebrate people who are moving forward. Every step forward is worthy of celebration, especially in a world where people are flaky, quitting left and right, abandoning ship, or living a complacent lifestyle.

However, taking steps forward can be met with opposition. When we deal with opposition and pushback in life, it can douse our fiery resolve. But it doesn't have to. In chapter 2, I talk about life's "blows." When life deals a major blow, each of us handles it differently.

How do you respond when life deals you a blow of betrayal, setback, or disappointment?

    A. Go crumbling to the ground
    B. Stumble, lose your footing
    C. It takes your breath away
    D. It leads you to prayer

I share how, over time, the blows have a lesser affect, especially if we are constantly drawing closer to Christ. I've learned that He is my hiding place and a very present help in time of need. However you react presently, my prayer is that over time you will see the fruit of drawing closer to God. You will feel the difference in your life. The newfound strength. You will soon begin to see, with your own eyes, how each new blow has a lesser affect. Furthermore, I pray you allow Father God to show you HOW He intends to use each of those fiery darts for your good. Yes, He can turn anything for your good!

> "We get knocked down but we are not destroyed." – 2 Corinthians 4:9 NLT

ACTIVATION

How will you move forward in this next season?

_____
_____
_____
_____
_____
_____
_____
_____

Ask Holy Spirit… **"What are the ditches the enemy keeps pulling me into? What 'blows' does he keep assaulting my life with and how do I overcome them? Show me how to recalibrate."** Write down whatever He shows you.

_____
_____
_____
_____
_____
_____
_____
_____

Week 1: Day 4

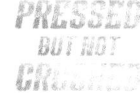

WHO IS GOD?

If I had a ministry that catered to new believers, I would probably give away gift bags with all kinds of relevant swag that includes a letter similar to the "Welcome Letter" found in chapter 3. As I mentioned in chapter 3, I imagine there are many different reactions that can come from such a letter.

How did you respond to the welcome letter on page 18?

    A. I AM SPARTA! "I was born ready!"
    B. Fight or flight risk. Side-eye reaction.
    C. Peace out! "Watch my smoke as I take off running."
    D. Other. Do tell…

Why do you think you reacted the way you did? How do you hope to react in the future?

_____
_____
_____
_____
_____
_____

So, now let's tackle our first piece of armor! The BELT of TRUTH! The Belt of Truth is FOUNDATIONAL. Without this foundation, the rest of the Christian walk is shaky at best.

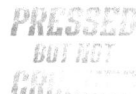

So, who is God? Let's look at some of the attributes covered beginning on page 22:

He's Good
He's Love
He's Gracious
He's Holy
He's Omnipotent
He's Omnipresent
He's Righteous
He's Sovereign
He's Omniscient

Which attribute caused the biggest reaction within you?

_____
_____
_____
_____
_____
_____
_____
_____

Whether it triggered you or reminded you of a testimony… if there was a negative reaction to any attribute, I encourage you to find all the scriptures associated with that attribute and war with them. Replace the lie in your mind with the truth by clinging to the Word.

"If God's highlighting an attribute, or if it's making you uncomfortable, this is an invitation to dive deeper."

Ask Holy Spirit, "What lies have I been believing concerning who God is?"

_____
_____
_____
_____
_____

When Holy Spirit exposes areas of our lives that do not align with His truth, there is only one step to take: Repent. It's that easy. You can bypass condemnation, you skip over self-pity, you can run over guilt. It just takes one step.

Prayer: God, I repent for not believing that You are _____. (Now war with the Word.) "The truth of the matter is that Your Word says you are (insert the supporting scriptures.) Father, keep me aligned with the Truth of who You are. Secure my Belt of Truth in this season and every season to come. In Jesus' Name, Amen."

I encourage you to get a copy of A. W. Tozer's *The Attributes of God* to help solidify you further into all truth.

Week 1: Day 5

WHO ARE YOU?

You are a child of the Most High King. Yes, you. He sent His son to die on a cross just for you. That's how valuable you are to Him. There's nothing you could ever do or say that will change His love for you.

I know… I know. That's a hard one for many people to fully embrace and accept. In this "cancel culture," God's unconditional love seems… unfathomable! Remember the pearl of great price in Matthew 13:45–46 (TPT)?

> "Heaven's kingdom realm is also like a jewel merchant in search of rare pearls. When he discovered one very precious *and exquisite* pearl, he immediately gave up all he had in exchange for it."

That pearl is you.

The enemy tries very hard to get us to disqualify ourselves from God's love. **Have you fallen into this trap?**

"Well I did _____ so I'm no longer loveable."

"I said _____ so He must no longer think I'm worthy."

STOP! Take these thoughts captive because they are imposters. Immediately replace the lie with the truth.

"Your identity is also NOT the things you may have done in your past. That is not who you are."

What part of the testimony, in chapter 5, resonated with you the most?

_____
_____
_____
_____
_____
_____

If there are any unresolved emotional hurts surrounding that, I want you to invite the Holy Spirit to minister healing to you today.

Ask Holy Spirit, **"What lies have I been believing concerning who I am or how God sees me?"**

_____
_____
_____
_____
_____

Prayer: God, this week, expose any lies I am believing concerning who I am in You. Show me the origin of the lies so I can extinguish them at the root! God, this week, remind me of who I am and how You see me. In Jesus' Name, Amen.

I encourage you to review prophetic words that have been spoken over you to be reminded of both (1) who you are and (2) how God feels about you.

ACTIVATION

WEEK 2

Chapters 6 – 7

We will spend all of week 2 unpacking our second piece of armor, The Breastplate of Righteousness, covered in chapters 6 and 7. Depending on how far you have gotten into the book, you've probably noticed a pattern with the breakdown of each piece of armor. We spend one chapter explaining *what* the purpose of the piece of armor is. Then we spend the next chapter assessing HOW to apply it practically, usually with a personal testimony.

The word of God has to be applied in our lives to make the most impact. Part of last week, we focused on the Belt of Truth. I pray by now you have become familiar with applying your Belt of Truth to your everyday life. Taking thoughts captive, as well as actively reminding yourself of the truth, is essential. The truth of who God is and the truth of who you are in Him.

So, now let's build upon our foundation with the Breastplate of Righteousness.

Week 2: Day 1

I open chapter 6 with a personal story about integrity. It starts with a nice meal at a restaurant, followed by an error on my bill that, had I not brought it to the attention of the waitress, would have "benefited" me. Listen, I love a discount! I love finding deals! Receiving perks, benefits, and favor make my day. However, I am not interested in receiving any of those things in a dishonest way.

Let's dissect this a bit more.

<u>Instant gratification vs. Delayed gratification:</u>

I submit to you that what you *think* you are getting away with in the <u>short term</u> may not be worth the long-term ramifications. Sure, had I kept my mouth shut I would have "saved" what? $2.50? $3? And walked away with a not so clear conscience.

What would you have done? Again, this is a safe place and there is no condemnation here, so be honest.

_____
_____
_____
_____
_____

What if there was a manager from my company there observing the whole scenario and a month later I'm put in front of this person for an interview? Do you see where I'm going with this? Ultimately, God sees everything and He rewards those He can trust. You see, God doesn't always approach us and say, "Well,

> "God sees everything. I believe that when we are faithful in the little things, He can trust us with bigger things...."

you know, I had this sweet gig set up for you. However, because you didn't pass the test, I will offer it to someone more trustworthy." No! You just miss out!

Some of those very prayers you're praying may be going unanswered because you have not been found righteous in a particular area of your life. I personally can't stand the thought of missing out on anything. What's worse is to *be* the very reason you are missing out. It is simply not worth it.

Choose to not succumb to anything that doesn't line up with the character of Jesus Christ. Choose to be righteous! It is so important to have a strong character in the midst of adversity. When the heat turns up, what's on the inside (any impurity) comes to the surface, just like gold being refined by fire.

Is there an area of your life where your integrity was recently tested? How did you do?

_____
_____
_____
_____
_____
_____
_____
_____

Prayer: God, I give you all the honor and glory for the times that I do get it right. Thank You for giving me the strength to do the right thing when I'm tested and tried. God, I repent for the times I've missed the mark. Give me the strength and strategy to make it right. In Jesus' Name, Amen.

ACTIVATION

I'm so grateful that God gives us the chance to try again and right any wrong. If there is someone you need to apologize to, do not hesitate to make amends. If you've taken something you shouldn't have, give it back. If you've been dishonest to someone, take the opportunity to go tell them the truth. Take a step in the right direction and watch how God will redeem you.

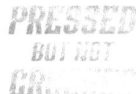

Week 2: Day 2

Righteousness comes at a price. You're going to have to sacrifice the instant gratification and sow into the bigger picture, the greater goal. But that's a way better price than sacrificing your conscience and character.

As believers, when we are heading down a wrong path, the Holy Spirit gives us warnings. When we give in to sin, these warnings were either ignored or they somehow went undetected. If they went undetected, it could be because a person was not alert or their conscience, over time, was seared.

We have a choice. If we take heed, it brings about a course correction. However, if we ignore or justify feeling and following our emotions, we embark on a conscience-searing process. That's very sobering.

Have you ever ignored the Holy Spirit's warning before?

_____
_____
_____
_____
_____

What did the warning feel/sound like?

_____
_____
_____
_____
_____

"I believe that when we participate in many actions that lack integrity, it begins to erode away at our conscience and our heart."

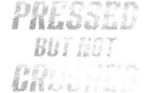

Make sure to pay attention to how Holy Spirit speaks to you. That way you can recognize His nudges in the future. These are the guardrails intended to keep you safe.

Let's talk about taking thoughts captive. It's great if you can put an unruly fire out before it burns the house down. But wouldn't it be better to prevent the fire from starting in the first place?

You've heard the saying, "Thoughts become words and words become actions." If we can squash the thoughts the enemy hits us with right away, that's best-case scenario.

Can you think of any negative/detrimental thoughts you could have squashed this week? Lustful thoughts? Thoughts that lacked integrity? Hateful thoughts?

_____

_____

_____

_____

_____

_____

_____

GREAT!! Let's squash them!

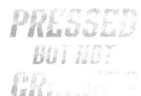

I will say this throughout this study - until you've memorized it and are saying it along with me. *This is a no condemnation zone!* Kick condemnation, self-pity, and guilt to the curb. Ain't nobody got time for that. We're doing surgery here. We're removing what is not like God.

These issues are not our identity or inheritance in life! It just takes a few simple steps.

- Identify it. ("Wow, that was a hateful thought!")
- Repent of it. ("God, forgive me for that horrible thought. I had a moment. I repent and choose to take that thought captive and throw it out. The truth of this situation is actually…")
- Ask God if there is a root issue that needs to be further addressed. ("Why am I feeling/acting this way right now? What triggered this? God, what lie am I believing about my life that has led me to this point? How can I prevent this from happening in the future? God, what is the truth so I can declare that over this situation?"). Ultimately, we don't want to be addressing only symptoms and not getting to the root of the issue. We also want to invite Holy Spirit to give us further revelation.

Declaration: A seared conscious in NOT my portion in Jesus' Name! I will yield to the "checks in my spirit" that the Holy Spirit sends. I will guard my heart, for out of it spring the issues of life. I put on my Breastplate of Righteousness today!

Week 2: Day 3

Today let's talk about willful disobedience. I know, I know… you can barely control your excitement, right? Remember when I decided to go on a shopping spree with my tithe money? Learn from my mistake. Willful disobedience… *no bueno*!

I know people who talk about growing up with parents who never discussed unpleasant topics in an attempt to "keep the peace." Say what now? I'm so glad God doesn't approach us that way. He warns us. He gives us tools to prepare us. He tells us to be alert. He sets us up for victory by making us aware of the pitfalls. Just take a read through the book of Proverbs. Doesn't it make more sense to warn people?

1 Peter 5:8 NLT warns, "Stay alert! Watch out for your great enemy, the devil He prowls around like a roaring lion seeking who he may devour."

The enemy is looking for an open door into your life because he's a legalist. He has already thoroughly examined God's law and he knows how to get legal right into your life. Disobedience and sin are his go-to entry points.

Check out the sample list of open doors below. These things puncture holes in your Breastplate of Righteousness.

Unforgiveness
Occult practices
Soul ties
Lying
Stealing
Adultery
Disobedience
Idolatry

> "Willful disobedience will remove God's hand of protection over certain areas, and the enemy is just waiting for a way in."

Fornication
Greed/coveting
Oppressing others
Shedding innocent blood

If you need to repent of anything on this list, then go for it. His mercies are new every single day. I am a big advocate for deliverance. One of the slyest deceptions the enemy has convinced the church of is that deliverance is not needed. Therefore, the body is walking around with a ton of "open doors" that are hindering their progress toward purpose and destiny.

Deliverance is basically throwing off anything that hinders, whether it gained access generationally or through you personally. I invite you to have a conversation with Holy Spirit about deliverance. In the meantime, let's repent for anything we have personally partnered with.

Repentance Prayer: God, I repent for wrongly participating in and partnering with _____. Forgive me and give me strength to never repeat it again in Jesus' Name.

Holy Spirit, if there is anything else not reflected on this list that I need to address, please reveal it to me. (Sit in silence to hear from Him.) What are the "holes" in my armor that need to be patched and which ones do I need to keep a close eye on?

_____
_____
_____
_____
_____
_____
_____
_____
_____

ACTIVATION

Week 2: Day 4

Now let's talk preventative maintenance!

What are some ways you can diligently try to guard your heart and, therefore, strengthen your breastplate?

Here are some suggestions. But as always, invite Holy Spirit into your personal process.

- Guard your tongue! Pause before responding to others, think before speaking. Very simple, but phenomenal strategy! Especially for those of us with a sharp tongue.

- When emotions flare up, stop and process with the Holy Spirit. Don't allow the enemy to drag you into presumption and assuming people's motives. "Holy Spirit, why do I feel this way?" is the best way to begin the process. Bringing your emotions into submission to your spirit is a daily discipline we should all practice. Again, don't allow the enemy to drag you around with your unchecked emotions.

- Be mindful of the things you entertain:
    - It should be a no-brainer that someone who struggles with alcoholism should not be hanging out at the bar. Protect yourself from your weaknesses and related temptations. This is not legalism, this is wisdom.
    - Remember, TRASH IN = TRASH OUT.
    - Everything is permissible but not all things are beneficial.

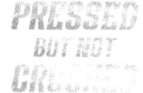

- I had a mentee who struggled with fornication. My suggestion to them was that maybe they should stop being alone in their apartment with their love interest. Is being alone with the person a sin? Of course not! It's permissible. But is being in that situation, while working on the fruit of the spirit of "self-control" and failing over and over again the best idea? It's a *no* for me. Is it beneficial? I think not.

- Stay out of gossip. This one is near and dear to my heart. If you know me or have followed me for any amount of time, you've heard me say that I am a *No Drama Zone*. One of the ways I maintain my peace (and that healthy boundary) is to keep my distance from gossipy people. These people also tend to know very minimal details about my personal life. Pay very close attention to those consistently sharing intimate details of other people's lives with you under the guise of "prayer requests." Avoid this trap like the plague. It's a slippery slope.

If you struggle in any of these areas, you already know what I'm going to say. Repent and do better. We're not taking any pitstops in Condemnation County or Guilt Township. It's that easy, that simple, and that powerful.

Which issue above do you struggle with the most? Ask Holy Spirit for your "preventative maintenance" strategy.

_____
_____
_____
_____

> *"'Smaller sins' that go unchecked lead to 'bigger sins.' This trap is a slippery slope devised by the enemy."* — Cassandra Bellevue

ACTIVATION

_____

_____

1 Corinthians 10:13 NLT says, "The temptations in your life are no different from what others experience."

Prayer: Father, as I make regular examinations of my Breastplate of Righteousness a lifestyle, please keep me sober and vigilant. Give me Your preemptive strategy for when I encounter any of the topics above and any other bait from the enemy. In Jesus' Name, Amen.

Week 2: Day 5

From victim mentality to victor mentality.

Of all the chapters in *Pressed But Not Crushed*, chapter 7 might be the one I've received the most reaction from. Everything from, "Wow!" to "You've got to be kidding me!" to "I don't know how you did it, girl." On and on and on. The sad part is, I'm not the only person who has encountered such a blatantly demonic scenario in a workplace environment. As a matter of fact, I personally know someone who walked through similar warfare on a much greater scale!

One of my biggest passions is debunking the lie that you are alone and you're the only one going through whatever it is you're facing. The enemy likes to try to isolate people and get them to come into agreement with his lies. Well, I'm here to tell you that you are not alone and you are not a victim.

You see, the posture of a victim is very different from the posture of a warrior, a victor. The enemy wants you to give up, sit down, shut up, and throw in the towel. Effectively removing you from the path toward fulfilling your destiny, calling, and purpose.

I was in a situation for a decade and a half where the enemy did everything in his power to try to convince me that someone else had the power to ruin my destiny. Furthermore, he wanted me to believe there was nothing I could do about it. He tried to convince me that I needed to retaliate and fight (from a place of fear and hopelessness).

He tried to tell me that I was all alone, didn't have a voice, and that God didn't care. He tried to brainwash me into thinking

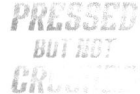

this "pharaoh" had all the power. When I think back on the situation now, I literally laugh out loud. The devil is a liar.

He was trying to get me to sabotage/ruin my Breastplate of Righteousness. He wanted me to lose my integrity and open doors/cross lines that would give him legal right and access into my life.

Have you encountered either scenario? Maybe a horribly toxic workplace scenario or a relationship that made you feel bound like a victim?

_____
_____
_____
_____
_____
_____

How did/are you handle(ing) it?

_____
_____
_____
_____
_____

In life's challenges, choose to go low. Process with the Holy Spirit. Ask Him how He would have you handle each situation. Going back to the Belt of Truth, solidify it in your heart that He's a just God and He will give you justice, whatever it looks like. In so doing, you keep your Breastplate of Righteousness in place and remain blameless.

You let Him fight for you. You make room for His strategy.

Purity of heart and integrity is key when it comes to righteousness. This will prevent us from being dragged down the road of our conscience being seared and developing a hardened heart. So get that breastplate secured! We won't be sacrificing our integrity and character to give in to our emotions, flesh, and lack of self-control.

Declaration: Thank You, Holy Spirit, that You go before me in every situation. You have my best interest at heart and You will guide me into all victory. Help me to make pleasing Your heart my #1 goal, God. I will stay in a place of righteousness today and every day because You have empowered me to do so. I am victorious in every situation, in Jesus' Name!

WEEK 3

Chapters 8 – 9

During week 3 we will do a dive into The Gospel of Peace Shoes.

When facing intense situations, it may seem impossible to "maintain our peace." BUT GOD! Listen, I'm trying to tell you, peace that surpasses all understanding is a REAL thing. I can't wait to share some newly acquired personal insight with you in my new book, *Radical Obedience*, that will be dropping in 2022. I could not be more excited!

I love that our God has a strategy for EVERYTHING! It makes me so happy to be cared for and protected that way. In case you've never heard it, or haven't heard it in a while…

> God loves you so much. He's a good Father and He cares about every single detail in your life. Yes, He is a God Who's very much into the details. Whatever is coming for your peace in this season, I rebuke and bind it in the mighty name of Jesus!

Join me this week as we continue to get strengthened in our inner man which, therefore, secures our armor. Thanks for hanging with me on this journey. It's so much better with company!

Week 3: Day 1

The main strategy to maintaining your peace during any trial is to *abide* in the face of fear. You've probably heard before that Satan is the *Father of Lies*. And he is the author of fear.

Have you ever been in a situation where you knew it was going to end badly, and it miraculously didn't? It's getting that voicemail notification and you immediately think, "Whoa, I'm totally getting fired," or "I'm sure he/she is mad at me," or "Surely, it's going to be a bad report." Most of us have done it.

Share a personal example of when fear tried to mar an experience for you, but, in the end, everything worked out.

_____
_____
_____
_____
_____
_____
_____
_____

I like to refer to these situations as "smoke and mirrors." The sense of fear and sense of doom feels so real in the moment. One of the tactics of the enemy is to get us to agree with the lie and therefore bring it into fruition. Almost like a self-fulfilling prophesy.

F.E.A.R. is False Evidence Appearing Real.

True story. I knew someone who was diagnosed with a medical condition. When they gave me the news something felt "off" in my spirit. This person immediately stepped into self-pity, claiming the condition as their own. They would make statements like, "I'll just have to deal with this for the rest of my life."

While I didn't have all the answers, I encouraged this person not to come into agreement with it. Not to claim the diagnosis and attach themselves to it, in their mind, or verbally. I encouraged them to have faith and believe God could turn the situation around. This is not stepping into denial, but I wanted them to speak life over their situation instead. I wanted them to start agreeing with God's word for healing. They were honest enough to admit they didn't have that level of faith. So, I encouraged them to, at the very least, STOP speaking death over themselves. Our words are powerful because we are created in God's image.

About a year later, this person had blood tests done with a new doctor, for a completely unrelated issue. When the results came back, the original "condition" was undetected. Confused, they asked the doctor to order another blood test. Same result. They requested a third set of blood tests. SAME RESULTS! The original condition no longer existed.

To date this person doesn't know what to believe. Did God heal them from this incurable condition? According to the doctor, it's possible this person NEVER had this condition in the first place. The current doctor said it could have been an error with the original lab test with the previous doctor.

Either way, do you see the importance of what you speak over your life when things get intense? Life and death are in the power of the tongue. What comes out of your mouth frames your world and frames your peace. **What are you speaking over yourself when you are battling fear?**

_____
_____
_____
_____
_____
_____
_____

What thoughts and agreements do you need to come out of alignment with today?

_____
_____
_____
_____
_____
_____
_____

Declaration: Father God, "May the words of my mouth and the meditation of my heart be pleasing to you, O LORD, my rock and my redeemer." (Psalm 19:14 NLT) Father, I repent for every negative word I have spoken over my situation. I come out of alignment with and rebuke the spirit of fear that is trying to take over my life. Help me to choose words carefully as to facilitate a lifestyle of peace.

Week 3: Day 2

Being stressed out is no fun. Living in fear is for the birds. There have been times in my life when my decisions made no sense to those around me. In those instances, they might have become accustomed to hearing me say, "I choose peace." Followed by, "You can't put a price on peace." It doesn't matter if the option I've chosen costs more money or takes me longer to accomplish, at the end of the day… I. CHOOSE. PEACE! Sometimes our peace is beyond circumstances we can control. What then? So glad you asked… *Abide!* Hit us with some truth, John:

> Remain in me, and I will remain in you. For a branch cannot produce fruit if it is severed from the vine, and you cannot be fruitful unless you remain in me. "Yes, I am the vine; you are the branches. Those who remain in me, and I in them, will produce much fruit. For apart from me you can do nothing. Anyone who does not remain in me is thrown away like a useless branch and withers. Such branches are gathered into a pile to be burned. But if you remain in me and my words remain in you, you may ask for anything you want, and it will be granted! When you produce much fruit, you are my true disciples. This brings great glory to my Father. – John 15:4-8 NLT

I don't know about you, but I'm gonna take a hard pass on the gather, pile, burn trajectory. I want to bear fruit. Particularly one of the fruits of the spirit which is … say it with me! PEACE! Scriptures are great, however, if we don't

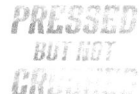

know how to apply them to our lives, we're kind of missing out!

What do you think are some practical ways to abide?

_____
_____
_____
_____
_____
_____
_____

When I get bad news, or my peace gets rattled, I find taking a moment to connect with God goes a long way.

- **Talking to God.** This can happen anywhere. That may sound like: "Jesus, help!" or "Father God, what do you say about this situation?"
- **Journal.** Write down how you're feeling and write whatever you hear Him saying in response.
- **Getting in the Word.** Find a scripture that addresses your issue. One that can anchor you in His peace.
- **Worship/Dance.** You can choose to start worshipping. That could be singing or opening your mouth and declaring how good God is.
- **Go for a hike.**

There are so many things you can do to connect with Him. Abiding can look so different for different people. I purposely listed a wide range of options to hopefully inspire you to find and explore more ways to connect with your Maker. Remember, He is Jehovah Shalom. God our peace.

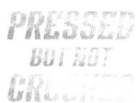

ACTIVATION

The next time you feel like your peace is being pushed out by anxiety, fear, or anger, what will your next step(s) be?

_____
_____
_____
_____
_____
_____

Prayer: Father God, Thank You for your peace that surpasses all understanding. When I choose to abide in You, I make room for You to deal with the other things contending for my peace. Help me to run to You first and foremost every time. In Jesus' Name, Amen.

Week 3: Day 3

Now let's talk about some shoes!!

When I was studying about the Roman soldiers' sandals, I was really impressed with the spikes on the bottom. The more I studied it out and focused on the functionality of the spike, I became even more intrigued. These spikes were good for taking and maintaining current ground and for acquiring new ground. There's so much spiritual application there. Let's dive in.

I don't know about you, but I don't like moving backwards. I want the fruit of my labor to remain. I like forward movement and momentum. Have you noticed that when we are not in a place of peace, we can become easily scattered mentally, spiritually, and/or emotionally? I've noticed that when I'm operating in fear, panic, or from a place of "crisis management," it's harder to hear Holy Spirit. I start grasping at straws and making decisions from an unsettled place. Sometimes those decisions move me backwards. If we're not careful to abide and settle those emotions, it can displace us from where we are standing.

I used the example of the mission trip to Guatemala in chapter 9. The mission God individually gave to the team of people I traveled with was very clear. But fear, chaos, confusion, bad reports, and fear of man was ultimately trying to derail us from our God-given mission.

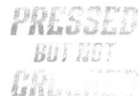

Have you ever experienced that? God gave you some marching orders and then it seemed like everything was coming against it? If so, what was the situation?

Were you able to push forward?

_____
_____
_____
_____
_____

What did you learn from that experience? Is there anything you would change if you could do it again?

_____
_____
_____
_____
_____

When I coach clients and they set off to do what God has called them to, they sometimes come back with reports of heightened spiritual warfare. My response to them is usually something like, "Sounds like you're on the right track!" The enemy is terrified of your forward progress so he's going to do whatever he can to slow you down or stop you altogether.

Ask Holy Spirit, "What is attempting to choke out my peace in this season? What is threatening my ability to abide and remain?"

_____
_____
_____
_____
_____

I want you to write down what Holy Spirit shows you and find scriptures that will anchor you in the future. (Example: If Holy Spirit is highlighting a spirit of fear, grab a scripture like Isaiah 26:3 and get grounded. Dig those sandals deeper into the terrain.)

_____
_____
_____
_____
_____

Declaration: Declare, "You will keep in perfect peace all who trust in you, all whose thoughts are fixed on you!" (Isaiah 26:3 NLT) Pray scripture. It's such a POWERFUL tool. We will dive deeper into that when we unpack the Sword!

ACTIVATION

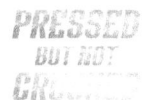

Week 3: Day 4

You have been activated.

Believe it or not, there is something you are doing, just completed, or going through in this season that is preparing you for your destiny. Let's talk about using your authority. God has really been driving this point home for me.

God doesn't waste our tears or our pain. Whatever you are walking through is more than likely an area He wants to not only give you victory in, but also, as you come through victoriously, He wants to give you authority over it.

I personally just walked through one of the **craziest** seasons of my entire life. The biggest lesson God was instilling in me was how to have peace in the midst of the unknown and in the chaos and when He seems silent. I can honestly say, coming out of that situation, that whatever situation hits me, I am able to maintain my peace in the midst of it. Watching, waiting, and praying.

It seems so simple, but let me tell you, it is much easier said than done. I had to daily lean into that discipline of abiding. And somewhere deep down, I KNEW that I had to pass these tests so that (#1) I didn't have to take those tests again, LOL, and (#2) so I could walk away with my authority in that given area. Now I see the evidence and the fruit of being able to navigate through great uncertainty with minimal emotionalism.

"What you're going through is your authority in the making."
– Cassandra Bellevue

In the past I would get angry and restless. In the past the enemy would try to suck me into a victim mentality. Or I'd play the, "What have I done wrong, God!?" game. Now I see He was training my hands for war and giving me authority over these challenging scenarios. Now I see how He sends people my way "randomly" who are fighting similar battles. Now I can give them the tools I gained in those experiences and encourage them to not give up or give in.

Ask ... "God, what area of my life/destiny are you training me for?"

_____
_____
_____
_____

"How am I doing?"

_____
_____
_____

"What should I focus more on?"

_____
_____
_____
_____

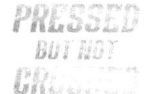

Prayer: God, show me how I can train in/break in my Gospel Shoes in this next season. Show me how to get activated in the work of the Gospel.

Week 3: Day 5

Oh, the gospel… That Good News! Jesus at the center, showcasing the love of the Father. Wow.

As Christians, we can get so familiar with the message of the gospel that it loses its wonder. Father, may we never lose our wonder. By the way, that is an excellent worship song, "Wonder" by Bethel Music and Amanda Cook. Check it out.

There are so many ways to spread the gospel. I've done street ministry, domestic mission trips, international mission trips, and marketplace Bible studies. I've been a Sunday School teacher, prophesied to random people in the grocery store, and lots of other things God has asked me to do. Yes, I've been that person prophesying by the mangos. I will become even more undignified than this. Once, while out of town, the Lord gave me an address, had me knock on the door and give a prophetic word to whoever answered the door. Yes, I did it, and pretty much ran away when I was done. LOL!

You see, sharing the gospel can take on many shapes and forms. It can be planned or spontaneous. However, the one constant is Jesus. I've been in church environments where sharing the gospel was treated like a quota. Evangelize five people a week, they said. It started to feel like legalism. But the peace that flows when you're sharing from a place of abiding cannot be surpassed. God opens the door and we just walk through. This Gospel brings peace and people need to hear it. Sharing from a place of peace can be your portion as well. Abide.

"In my heart I knew I was called to this, and I felt that supernatural peace that surpasses understanding the Bible speaks of."

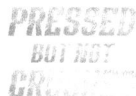

How do you feel about sharing the gospel …

… With unsaved friends?

_____
_____
_____
_____
_____

… With strangers?

_____
_____
_____
_____
_____

If you struggle, why?

_____
_____
_____
_____
_____

I want you to know that wherever God sends you with this Gospel, peace is your portion. And for those you share it with, who readily receive it, peace is their portion as well. Peace to take on any and every situation.

Ask Holy Spirit, "How do I practically apply the Shoes of the Preparation of the Gospel of Peace to my life? What is one step I can take today?"

_____
_____
_____
_____
_____
_____
_____
_____

This Gospel is life-changing, my friends. We carry the very key to unlock so many from their personal prisons – Jesus Christ. Let's strap on these shoes, stand our ground in our own walk, and take ground by helping others step into Freedom and Peace.

ACTIVATION

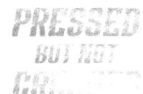

Week 4

Chapters 10 – 11

I've stayed fascinated by this fun fact concerning the Armor of God. Every piece goes on and stays on except for two pieces. This week we'll focus on one of them, the Shield of Faith.

It's so interesting to me that our faith protects us … it's the Shield of Faith. Standing on our faith, faith in who God is, the calling on our life personally, our faith in the infallible word of God, and the promises God has made to us … being steadfast and unwavering in our faith protects us from the fiery darts of the enemy. It represents our shield in the upright position … ACTIVATED! What a picture!

I mentioned in the book how I always envision that the inside of my shield of faith is inscribed with of all the things I have faith in. So when the hits keep coming, when they're coming in hot, when the pressure is mounting, what I believe in is ever before my eyes.

I don't want to live in an "out of sight, out of mind" reality. I want the things I have faith in and for to be locked and loaded in my line of sight!

What are you standing in faith believing? Are they fresh in your mind? Can you recite the scriptures, can you quote the

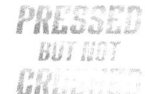

prophetic promises, are you steadily activating your faith in the midst of your battle?

Either way, we're going to explore some additional practical steps that will lead us down the path to victory, shields lifted high! Are you ready?

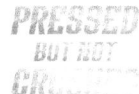

Week 4: Day 1

According to Webster's dictionary, "Faith is the complete trust and confidence in something."

Faith is such a ginormous topic to tackle. However, we are going to break it up into chunks over the course of this week. So let's start with a question for you. It's a deep one, so take your time and don't rush through it.

What are some things you have complete faith in? What do you have complete trust and confidence in? (i.e. your make-up routine, your truck, your boss, that the food will be great at your favorite restaurant)

_____
_____
_____
_____
_____

Was God on that list?

_____
_____
_____
_____
_____

If not, why? Be honest. Remember this is a no condemnation zone. We can't work on areas of our life that need to change if we don't first identify there's an issue to begin with. I find that personal growth requires us to be real with ourselves and let go of the churchy Sunday School answers.

If God wasn't on your list, why was that the case?

_____
_____
_____
_____
_____

Your faith is what will protect you from many of the fiery darts of the enemy. It's imperative that we examine how ironclad our faith is and make the appropriate adjustments.

Ask Holy Spirit to help you with this self-check. "Holy Spirit, on a Scale of 1 – 10, how strong is my faith? What specific areas of my faith do you want me to take a closer look at and strengthen this week?"

_____
_____
_____
_____
_____

Write down whatever He says and dedicate some time this week to get His strategy for moving forward.

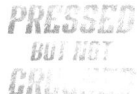

Prayer: Father, thank You for being faithful. Help me to be faithful like you. Strengthen my Shield in the days to come for your glory!

Week 4: Day 2

I always like to remind people:

If we say we have faith in something, our actions become the lie detector, if you will.

Do you remember those "trust fall" challenges we used to do as kids? Where you'd close your eyes and fall backwards, assuming the person you claimed to trust would *actually* catch you? If I say I trust someone completely, and they invite me to do one of those "trust fall" challenges, my acceptance of the challenge either proves I trust them or suggests that I don't.

There are many ways to put faith into action. One example is a prophetic act. Have you ever engaged in a prophetic act? It's basically when you take action concerning something God has promised you. It doesn't mean that you are jumping ahead of Him or taking control. It is simply a gesture that communicates you're onboard, you choose to believe Him, and you're not afraid to show it.

I remember one time someone prophesied over me that God was going to be opening up doors for me concerning a particular area of my life. I was lying down when she told me that, but something in me made me jump out of the bed and take a giant step forward through one of the open doors in my house! It was my way of saying, "Yes, God! I hear you and I accept the invitation. By faith, and as a prophetic act, I am taking a step through whatever door You open for me."

Think of faith as a verb. Faith is ACTION! Faith has no middle ground.

Another time someone prophesied over me that I was crossing over into a season of financial blessing and overflow. So, you know what I did? I opened an extra savings account! LOL. Some may find that silly but that was my way of saying, "Yes, God! I believe you will bless me financially and I'm going to open this account by faith in order to house the financial overflow that's coming!" This was a prophetic act but also a practical way to prepare for what I was already asking for in prayer.

What are you believing God for in this season? How are you activating your faith concerning His promise?

_____

_____

_____

_____

_____

_____

_____

Prayer: Holy Spirit, show me how to partner with You and how to prophetically step out concerning the promises You've spoken over my life, in Jesus' Name!

Week 4: Day 3

You know, it's usually when we step out and decide we're all in that the enemy makes his move. When we choose to believe God for His promises and posture ourselves for all He has for us, that's when it comes. The counterattack. The devil doesn't want you to move forward. Remember his agenda is to steal, kill, and destroy. His strategy is all about setbacks, hindrances, and trying to take your knees out from under you however he can. And you know what else? He fights dirty.

The kingdom of darkness, hell, is all about death and hopelessness. Did you catch that? Hopelessness. Do you remember the biblical definition of faith? Hebrews 11:1 NKJV says, "Now faith is the substance of things HOPED for, the evidence of things unseen."

On Page 76 of *Pressed But Not Crushed*, I list a few types of fiery darts the enemy tends to send our way. **Which fiery dart is he hitting you with the hardest in this season?**

_____
_____
_____
_____
_____
_____

Doubt? "Did I hear God correctly?"
Shame? "You can't step into your calling after everything you've done!"

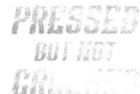

Lies? "God has completely abandoned me."
Despair? "Nothing is ever going to change."
Comparison? "Look how much more accomplished and successful they are than you."

What are some other fiery darts the enemy comes at you with?

_____
_____
_____
_____
_____
_____
_____

I believe identifying patterns of attack will be very helpful to your battle plan. One thing that I have also noticed in my walk is that patterns of attack can also point to destiny and purpose.

Are you constantly being hit in the area of your finances? It could it be that you are called to transfer wealth for God's kingdom, to fund His purposes. Think of Dave Ramsey's personal testimony. This man was a millionaire and lost is all. He had to rebuild his wealth from scratch! His journey and the things he learned along the way are now the tools and principles he teaches others to help them build their own wealth!

Are you constantly being hit with infirmity? Maybe you are called to the ministry of healing? Think of John G. Lake's testimony. This man was used mightily by God in the area of healing.

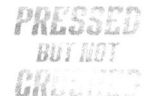

What most people don't realize is that he battled on the front lines against the spirit of infirmity that attacked himself and his family. That's where his faith was built. That's where his authority was cultivated.

Do you deal with major self-esteem issues and fear of speaking? It's quite possible God is calling you to the forefront to be a voice and the enemy is trying to shut you down prematurely. Remember Moses? Exodus 4:10 NLT states, "But Moses pleaded with the LORD, 'O Lord, I'm not very good with words. I never have been, and I'm not now, even though you have spoken to me. I get tongue-tied, and my words get tangled.'"

We're going to ask Holy Spirit to help you identify the lies and the patterns over the next few days. However, for the lies you identified today, let's go after them! **What categories did they fall in?**

_____
_____
_____
_____
_____

Prayer: Thank You, God, for exposing the enemy and showing me the chinks in my armor. Today I commit to pushing back by stepping into alignment with Your truth by faith. I take the lie that _____ and replace it with the truth that _____. I am victorious in this area, in Jesus' mighty name!

ACTIVATION

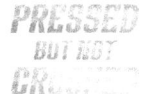

Week 4: Day 4

Let's face it. If we are going to do better, reach higher, and commit to progress, there are things that we are going to have to leave behind.

One lesson I keep learning over and over is that, with every new season, some things are going to shift. When things shift, not everything that you are currently traveling with can come with you. Sometimes it's a hobby. Sometimes it's a job. Sometimes it's a friendship. It is VERY important when you are battling in the area of faith what voices you allow in your ears!

I share in chapter 10 how in one season the Lord had me believing for a new job, and one wrong voice in my ear almost made me give up on that promise! We need to be mindful of who and what we are listening to, and trash anything that is coming against the things God has called us to have faith for.

How are you going to change the voices in your life (email subscriptions, podcasts, social media followings)? Let's do a quick activation. **Holy Spirit, which voices am I accommodating/have access to me that need to be removed from my life?**

_____
_____
_____
_____

_____

_____

Was what He spoke to you surprising?

_____

_____

_____

_____

_____

So, we're removing the negativity and we're going to pump our lives full of more things that increase our faith. **What are five things that cause faith to rise in your life?**

_____

_____

_____

_____

_____

In *Pressed But Not Crushed* I share a few examples of things that can increase your faith.

1. Worship Music
2. Praying prayers out of one of my favorite prayer books, *Prayer Rain*
3. Fellowshipping with fiery friends who speak life and always have a testimony on their lips.

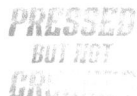

4. Listening to encouraging sermons (podcasts, social media)
5. Rereading my prophetic words

Did any of those strategies resonate with you? If so, which one(s)?

_____
_____
_____
_____
_____

Let's solidify your strategy with Holy Spirit now!

Holy Spirit, what things/activities/people should I incorporate in my life to help me increase my faith in this season?

_____
_____
_____
_____
_____
_____
_____

Prayer: God, thank You that You have not left us to figure this all out on our own. The strategy for everything in life resides in You. Show me how to increase my faith. In Jesus' Name I pray.

Week 4: Day 5

I want to kick off today with a fun fact. As I re-read that job loss testimony starting on page 78 of *Pressed But Not Crushed*, I realize I am currently in a job making - just shy of - 3 times the salary that "dream job" offered. I share that to brag on God. He takes us from glory to glory, praise God! And you want to know something even crazier? The *same* situation repeated itself seven years later. Not even joking! Got a verbal job offer right before the pandemic and a couple months later they reneged. Like many companies, during that time, they were now laying off employees.

I can tell you, the second time around I was standing in a place of greater faith and much more expectancy than the first time. Sometimes we go through similar situations and the enemy tries to convince us that we are not progressing. He tries to tell us that, just like the children of Israel, we're just wandering around the desert and circling the base of the mountain. However, you know what God showed me? You may be circling the mountain, but it is not what it appears to be. The enemy is great at throwing smokescreens and mirrors and trying to convince us our situation is one way when it's not. That's why it's so important to invite Holy Spirit to help us see with a new set of eyes.

Going around the mountain can mean circling the base of the mountain, retracing the same steps, and making no progress. But I submit to you, there's another way you can be going around the mountain that's actually positive. What if you were following a path around the mountain that was taking you higher? As you trek up and around the mountain, you may see some similar sights, yes. However, each time you are standing at a higher vantage point, right?

Just because you may be seeing the same scenery doesn't always mean you're in the same place. Sometimes God's trying to show you how far, or how high, you've come. You're "seated" in a different place as you stand your ground in a similar battle. God is showing you your higher authority. And that's what He did for me. This time as I dealt with a job being "robbed" from me, I couldn't help but hear the lyrics to the worship song "Do it Again." It talks about seeing God move the mountains. Now that we've seen it, we have faith to believe He will do it again! That's faith in action. No matter what it looks like, no matter the lie, SHIELDS UP!

What is the "impossible" promise you are believing for, by faith, in this season?

_____
_____
_____
_____
_____
_____
_____

Which situation from the past can you pull from? Is there one that will raise your faith for your current situation?

_____
_____
_____
_____
_____

Ask Holy Spirit, "What can I declare and decree over my situation to help keep my shield up?"

_____
_____
_____
_____
_____

ACTIVATION

May your faith muscle continue to grow as you hold up that Shield of Faith, unwavering and refusing to allow any of those fiery darts to set you back! In Jesus' Name, Amen!

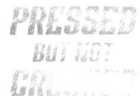

Week 5

Chapters 12 – 13

Oh, how God wants us to be secure in our salvation and in everything His salvation brings.

Can you imagine giving someone a gift card for a million dollars but they never use it because they don't trust its validity or value?

Sometimes, if we aren't careful, we can wind up doing this with the gift of salvation … and even our helmet of salvation. This helmet, as we will explore more thoroughly, is about the hope of our salvation and all the promises that come with it. These are things that automatically become part of our inheritance the second we accept Christ as our Savior. They are some of the more obvious things like the promise of heaven.

But what about some of the promises that are ours for the taking in the "land of the living?" Believe it or not, there are things that belong to us here. He has work for us to do here. There are blessings and rewards that He wants us to experience here on this earth. He has plans, promises, and purposes He desires to partner with us concerning. Right here, right now!

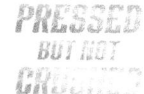

This is the stuff the enemy wants us to miss. However, I'm here to highlight several of these items that are the "hope of our salvation" so we'll go after them with zeal!

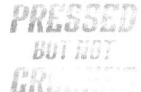

Week 5: Day 1

Today I want to focus in on a sobering topic I spoke about in chapter 12 of *Pressed But Not Crushed*: the Spiritual bulimia/anorexia analogy. I remember the first time I heard the analogy, it rocked me. Holy Spirit speaks to me a lot through pictures, word pictures, dreams, visions, and analogies. So this bulimia/anorexia analogy has stuck with me for years. So much so I added it to the book.

One of the reasons it had such a profound impact on my life is because there was a person, in my close circle, that I could see this principle working through. Based on the analogy, this person was a spiritual bulimic. Before seeing this concept play out with my own eyes, I would have had a hard time believing that someone could know so much of the Bible and not be a faithful Christian. But here I was watching that very paradigm shift being played out before me.

Some of us may know it as head knowledge versus heart knowledge. God's Word is not like the middle school midterm we cram for and then do a brain dump after we take the test. It's not God's will for any of us to not be filled and nourished by His Word.

Have you ever found yourself in either ditch?

_____
_____
_____
_____
_____

Do you know someone in either ditch?

_____
_____
_____
_____
_____

The purpose of this exercise/examination is not to make anyone feel bad or to judge others. However, we need to do a self-check and let's be real, sometimes it's easier to see our vices when we see them played out in someone else's life. Tell me I'm not the only one who sees a habit in someone else and Holy Spirit speaks to your heart, "Yeah… that's what it looks like when you do it, too." Haha. It doesn't always feel good, but He chastises those He loves. Never forget that.

If you are not sure, ask Holy Spirit:

"Do I show any signs of being a 'spiritual bulimic' or a 'spiritual anorexic'? If so, what are they?"

_____
_____
_____
_____
_____
_____

ACTIVATION

"Do I walk through life with a ton of head knowledge that fails to actually transform my life for the better? What are these areas and how can I cultivate a tangible transformation?"

_____
_____
_____
_____
_____

"Am I seeing little to no lasting transformation in my personal life? What is the root cause of this pattern?"

_____
_____
_____
_____
_____

"When was the last time I got in the Word to encounter the Father?"

_____
_____
_____
_____
_____

"Am I making time to feast on His Word on a regular basis? How can I be more intentional?"

_____
_____
_____
_____
_____

Whatever He highlighted or revealed, I want you to press in. Go even deeper. If Holy Spirit told you were in a good place, rejoice! Praise Him and ask Him to keep you rooted and grounded in His Word.

If He highlighted areas of opportunity, ask Him for His strategy. The last thing we want to do here is to fall into legalism and religious rules. Instead, **ask Holy Spirit what His strategy is to get you on the right track.** For the 'spiritual anorexic' it may be to find a devotional covering a topic you're excited or curious about. Or it may simply be to start by reading a Proverb a day.

Fun fact: In July 2021, the Lord led me to read through the book of Proverbs on social media. I read just one chapter a day. You can find those videos on either my YouTube, Facebook, or Instagram page if you want some company on your journey.

> "The good news is He isn't looking for perfection."

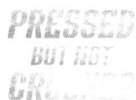

If the Holy Spirit highlighted that you may be leaning towards the 'spiritual bulimia' category, ask Him how you can make the Word come alive in your life. Ask Him how you can retain it unto transformation. Write it down.

_____
_____
_____
_____
_____
_____
_____
_____
_____
_____
_____
_____

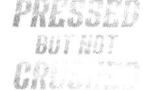

Week 5: Day 2

Let's talk about salvation!

I recently was teaching a 4th-5th grade Sunday school class when these little 10- and 11-year-old scholars tried to get all SUPER theological on me with all their "But what if" questions. I wanted to yell, "YOU CAN'T HANDLE THE TRUTH!" like I was in a "A Few Good Men." However, the truth is they can handle it. LOL.

Jesus said in Matthew 18:4 NLT, "I tell you the truth, unless you turn from your sins and become like little children, you will never get into the Kingdom of Heaven."

The gospel is simple. Yet there are many voices who want to overcomplicate it. What I explained to the kids was the simple gospel, and when they threw me another "what if," I gave them the simple Gospel again. My pastor refers to the "Jesus Plus" program a lot when he preaches. He's referring to this perverted ideology where Salvation = Jesus + _____. You see some of that trying to permeate the early church and Paul came for it, specifically to squash it. It's simply Jesus. Repent of your sins and make Him Lord of your life. That is salvation. That's it. There's no "Plus" program. Jesus plus works? No. Jesus plus Seminary? No. Jesus plus whatever new fad nonsense hits the church culture? NO!

I told these kids to imagine a canyon. There is a wide chasm. We are on one side, God is on the other. Now picture Jesus on the cross. He is resurrected and that cross is laid across the chasm, across the separation.

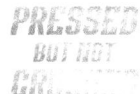

We walk across it like a bridge to God when we repent of our sins and accept Him as Lord. Jesus is the bridge. The Way. The Truth. The Life. That's it.

Do you still struggle with the lie of the enemy that says, "That's too easy!"?

_____
_____
_____
_____
_____

Re-read the "Am I saved testimony" starting on page 93. **When have you ever experienced feeling that way?**

_____
_____
_____
_____
_____

Do you constantly struggle with the question of "am I really saved or not?" We can shut that down today if you care to join me.

_____
_____
_____
_____
_____

Ask the Holy Spirit, "Have I accepted Jesus Christ as my Lord and Savior?" What did He tell you?

_____
_____
_____
_____
_____
_____
_____
_____

ACTIVATION

If He said yes, then pray the following prayer:

> "God, I bind double-mindedness today and I rest securely in my salvation. I have said yes to Jesus. You have accepted me and my salvation is sealed."

If He said no, then pray the following prayer if you would like to invite Jesus to be Lord of your life:

> "Father, thank You for making the ultimate sacrifice for me. I want to repent of living life on my own terms and of sin that I have partaken in. Forgive me. Today I surrender my life, ask Jesus into my heart, and ask Him to be Lord of my life. Amen"

I declare and decree that God is not the author of confusion. You will stand firm and secure in your salvation today and forever more. In Jesus' Name, Amen!

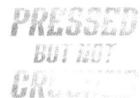

Week 5: Day 3

Now that we are clear on salvation and where we each stand individually, let's focus. Imagine someone getting ready to go for a run. They kneel down and tie their shoes, stand back up and stick their head inside their shirt.

Wait, what?

Oh, is that not how you imagined that scene ending. Maybe you expected to see the runner look up and scope the road they were about to take on. That would make more sense, wouldn't it? Then why do many people get saved and then get trapped in "navel gazing?"

Wow. That's the enemy trying to render us useless and make us hopeless.

When putting on your Helmet of Salvation, I believe you are putting on *the hope of your salvation.*

Take a look at the list on page 100. You guessed it. Time for an Activation!

I'm heavy on the activations because, as believers, we must get comfortable connecting with our Maker. Communing with Him *has* to become second nature. It is not a priest, prophet, pastor, or anyone else's job to be a steady liaison facilitating you having a conversation with God. They can give you nuggets to jump start a conversation, but you must get comfortable speaking to Him and listening to Him. Spoiler alert: That's a relationship!

Of the various "hopes" listed on page 100, which one jumps out at you, making you feel hopeless?

_____
_____
_____
_____
_____
_____

For example, the first one says, "knowing your future is secure in Christ." **When you read that, does it make you feel sad because your hope barometer (if there was such a thing) is low?** Well, that's great! It's great because you've just identified an area that needs the Father's touch and your agreement.

Holy Spirit, show me which items on the list of 'hopes' you want to work on with me this week. Holy Spirit, if I'm "naval gazing", help me to lift my head and focus on the race set before me. Show me what I'm not seeing that my hope may be renewed. List them here.

_____
_____
_____
_____
_____
_____

ACTIVATION

If you have multiple items on that list that did not make you feel hopeful, maybe attack one a week. Yes, you can continue working on this stuff even *after* the six weeks is over. Commit to getting to a point where you read the entire list and shout for joy because you really believe and now your hope is running high!

Week 5: Day 4

Now, I'll be honest. There are times when your hope may waver. You know, those times when our eyes are on the "wind and waves" and not on Jesus. When you identify one of those moments, I encourage you not to start beating yourself up. You simply have to recalibrate.

What are some specific things you can do when things come against the hope of your salvation? How do you block them?

_____

_____

_____

_____

_____

I suggested that you can do some of the following:
- Read some of your prophetic words.
- Read journal entries of the things God has spoken concerning your life and destiny.
- What does scripture say is the hope of our salvation? Do a biblical word search for hope. What do you find?
- If you have gone blank, ask God to tell you again, "What is the HOPE of my salvation?"

I want you to make a list of things that are the hope of your salvation. Write down as many as you can.

"Wherefore gird up the loins of your mind, be sober, and hope to the end for the grace that is to be brought unto you at the revelation of Jesus Christ." - 1 Peter 1:13 KJV

You may have to come back and add to this list time and time again as you think of new things.

_____
_____
_____
_____
_____
_____
_____
_____
_____
_____
_____

Holy Spirit, reveal to me the "Hope of my Salvation." He may show you a word, a picture, speak a word, speak a sentence to you, or highlight a scripture. Just write it down.

_____
_____
_____
_____
_____
_____
_____

Week 5: Day 5

When we launched the first *Pressed But Not Crushed* Bible Study in the Spring of 2021, our group met online every Wednesday night for six weeks. I remember one night when we were focusing on the Helmet of Salvation, Holy Spirit gave me a prophetic word for the group. He said…

"I want to mesmerize my children with hope."

As simple as that sounds, I sat there stunned, feeling the presence of the Holy Spirit. I'm a word nerd. So when the Lord uses me to prophesy, or when He's personally speaking words to me, I go look up the definition of the words. Believe it or not, I do this even for words that I'm familiar with because I find that the official definition always provides way more context, insight, and revelation.

The word mesmerize means to "hold the attention of (someone) to the exclusion of all else or so as to transfix them." Now re-read the prophetic word with that definition in mind. It hits differently, doesn't it? The heart of the Father is to hold our attention. He wants us to be so transfixed with Him, and the hope of our salvation in Him, to the exclusion of all else. Wow!

My prayer for you today is that you would be mesmerized with the hope that can only be found in the Father. He's a good Father. He has a plan to prosper you and not to harm you. He has a hope and a future for you. (Jeremiah 29:11)

"No one can snatch you from God's Hand. That's the hope of your salvation right there. Rest assured in it!"

"Wherefore gird up the loins of your mind, be sober, and hope to the end for the grace that is to be brought unto you at the revelation of Jesus Christ." - 1 Peter 1:13 KJV

There is only one entity that would want to distract you from all that goodness. Only one sinister being who would have you question your salvation. Only one deceiver who would have you focusing on and chasing anything other than what God has for you.

So deal the ultimate TKO blow to this enemy by choosing to be mesmerized by Father God today and every day.

Holy Spirit, expose some things in my life that may be robbing me from being mesmerized by You?

_____
_____
_____
_____
_____

What can I do to stay in this place of being mesmerized?

_____
_____
_____
_____
_____

Prayer: My prayer over you: "God release dreams/night visions to show your people the hope of their salvation in You. I bind and sever everything that is coming against the hope of the one reading this prayer. Renew minds and activate them in this area of hope today, in Jesus' Name!"

Write down anything God may be speaking to your heart:
_____
_____
_____
_____
_____
_____
_____

ACTIVATION

Week 6

Chapters 14 – 17

This week we are going to tackle our last piece of armor, the Sword of the Spirit, as well identify specific "fiery darts" that can trap us.

So the sword might be my favorite piece. Don't tell the other pieces of armor I told you that. There are so many amazing fun facts about the sword. One of my favorites is the fact that you activate it by holding it up. Does dragging a sword around behind you do you any good? Your sheath is great for bringing your sword to the battle, however, if you don't pull the joker out fast enough when the enemy engages, then what?

There are many things that can happen if you don't hold it up. There are also many things that can happen if you don't keep it up!

Oh, the POWER of the Sword, which is God's word. I can never fully express how grateful I am to God for His word. I want to digest as much of it as I can, while I can. There is no promise the Bible won't be banned in the future here in America. Other countries have already taken those drastic measures.

The sword is something that is most effective when it's *in action*! One of my personal goals is to memorize more of it, not for bragging rights, but for it to be deep-seated in my heart. That

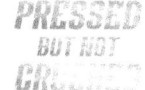

way I can pull on it whenever I need it. Thank You, God! Let's talk about this in even more detail on the following pages.

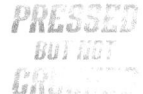

Week 6: Day 1

My favorite fact about the Sword of the Spirit is this: In our entire armory, the sword is the only *offensive* weapon. Take some time to review the other pieces if you need to. Am I right or amirite? Everything is defensive in function. The sword is what God has given us to take out our enemy. Father God is a mastermind. He is a God that is intimately involved with *all* the details of our lives. So imagine this with me. He came up with the Armor of God and the one offensive weapon He gave us is HIS WORDS!

Can I get a mic drop on this!? HIS WORDS, people! That is so unbelievably amazing to me. I cannot stop being excited about it! HIS WORDS! Haha.

I shared an experience of watching my kid playing a video game one day. It starts on page 105 of *Pressed But Not Crushed*. What I was actually observing was him playing a game of hide and seek, because remember, he had no weapons.

Do you ever feel that way in real life? Like you're in the middle of an intense battle and you have no weapon to help you advance? So, instead of being proactive and pushing forward, you hide? Or you abdicate from whatever position God placed you in, therefore bailing on your responsibilities?

_____
_____
_____
_____

What was/is that situation?

_____
_____
_____
_____
_____

Listen, the enemy has been found out! It's time to give him his eviction notice! The Word of God is ALIVE, ACTIVE, LIVING, BREATHING, AND POWERFUL! **Now if you really believed that with all of your heart, how would you be waging war today? No, seriously, what would you do today if you believed that 100%?**

_____
_____
_____
_____

I'd personally be looking up any scriptures that talk about victory or about the subject matter I'm dealing with. **I want you to find three scriptures about being victorious in Christ. List them below.**

_____
_____
_____
_____
_____

"...and God hath chosen the weak things of the world to confound the things which mighty." - 1 Corinthians 1:27b KJV

Now find three more scriptures that address whatever battle you're facing (financial, relational, sickness, etc.) What are God's promises concerning this area?

_____
_____
_____
_____
_____
_____
_____
_____

ACTIVATION

We're not playing games with the enemy today (or any day for that matter). We either believe God at His word or we don't.

Consistency is key as well. Speak His word as often as you can. Make flash cards and swap them out each month. Put them up all around your house. Whatever you're comfortable with. But take action!

Prayer: Holy Spirit, show me how to wield my sword in this season. Give me a picture that captures how we're going to move forward in this season.

Week 6: Day 2

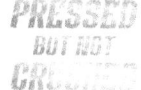

Have you ever heard of an anchor word or an anchor verse? Sometimes when we are going through a challenging season, God will give us a prophetic word that is spoken to help anchor us in the season we're facing. It's usually an encouraging word to remind you God is with you and what His promise is.

Several years ago, I was fighting one of the most difficult battles of my entire life. That season lasted over a decade. There were several scriptures God kept speaking over me in my personal time with Him. Also, many prophetic words I "randomly" received from ministers included these scriptures without them having any foreknowledge of the significance.

One of them was Galatians 6:9 NLT, "So let's not get tired of doing what is good. At just the right time we will reap a harvest of blessing if we don't give up." This scripture would often be prophesied on a day when I felt ready to give up. Every time I heard that verse, it was like a kiss from heaven reminding me of two things: (1) God had not forgotten or forsaken me. He saw me and He was also with me. (2) His promise to me was that if I didn't give up He'd reward me greatly, and I am living out some of that "harvest blessing" even today! But when I wanted to quit and agree with the spirit of death over my situation, God came to my rescue to speak life. Eventually He brought in the supernatural power that shifted that situation for my good and His glory. Praise His Holy Name!

Because His word is active, living, breathing, and powerful, it hits much different than words written in a novel or a newspaper. Do you young'uns even know what a newspaper is?

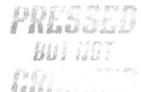

Hebrews 4:12 NLT says, "For the word of God is alive and powerful. It is sharper than the sharpest two-edged sword, cutting between soul and spirit, between joint and marrow. It exposes our innermost thoughts and desires."

It's ALIVE. It's not dead. It's full of LIFE. Life defines something that has "the capacity for growth, reproduction, functional activity, and continual change preceding death." God's Word can speak life over you, over your situation, over your loved ones, and over the desires of you heart.

It's POWERFUL. It's not weak and complacent. The definition of power says, "the capacity or ability to direct or influence the behavior of others or the course of events."

What areas of your life can stand to benefit from supernatural life and power. Write them down.

_____

_____

_____

_____

_____

_____

_____

_____

Prayer: God, I lift these areas before you and I step into my God-given authority to affect change. Show me when my speech and actions become contrary to Your will. Course correct me when I step out of alignment with You. Put the right scripture in my mouth and at the right time bring about a victorious result in Jesus' Name. I trust You, God. In Jesus' Name I pray, Amen.

ACTIVATION

Week 6: Day 3

These last three days, I want to address the specific areas of pressing I touched on in *Pressed But Not Crushed*. There are lot of other areas of pressing, so this is by no means an exhaustive list. However, I've seen these up-close and personal and would love to share some lessons I've learned while walking through them or observing them in others.

In Chapter 16, we unpacked rejection. I honestly don't know that there is a believer out there who has not been touched by this one. Rejection comes in all shapes, modes, and forms, and is experienced at different levels of impact.

When rejection hits you personally, what are the lies the enemy tries to follow it up with in your life?

_____
_____
_____
_____
_____

Which part of Leah's story (Genesis 29-35) hit a little too close to home for you?

_____
_____
_____
_____
_____

What else in the Rejection chapter resonated with you? Which quote(s), scripture(s), or paragraph spoke to you?

_____
_____
_____
_____
_____
_____
_____
_____

Well, news flash! You are accepted by your Creator. Not only does He accept you, He created you, molded you, and stamped you with purpose, calling, and destiny.

Now, of all the ways the God has accepted you into His Family (Birth, Marriage Adoption), which one impacted you the most and why?

_____
_____
_____
_____
_____
_____
_____

"Have you noticed that God has invited us into His family in every way you can join a family in the natural?"

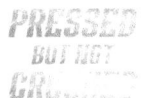

ACTIVATION

Ask Holy Spirit, "Where were You during those times I felt rejected?"

_____
_____
_____
_____
_____

Now ask Holy Spirit, "What were You speaking over me in those situations? What are you speaking over me today?"

_____
_____
_____
_____
_____
_____

Prayer: Holy Spirit, I believe you were there. Thank You for those life-breathing words that you were speaking over me. May Your words resound louder than all the other voices and all the other lies.

Week 6: Day 4

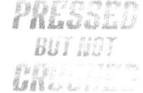

Ohhhh complacency. Now I haven't personally dealt with this one, but boy have I seen it in operation up close and personal.

In chapter 17, we take a closer look at complacency. Now remember, say it with me, this is a no condemnation zone. So, as you dive deeper and work though this with Holy Spirit, we are not taking a "woe is me" stance but an "I am Sparta" stance. Be determined to shred everything not like God and move on.

I still remember how stunned I was when Holy Spirt spoke that to my heart. It's very sobering, isn't it?

Dictionary.com's definition of complacency is, "a feeling of quiet pleasure or security, <u>often while unaware of some potential danger, defect, or the like; self-satisfaction or smug satisfaction with an existing situation, condition, etc.</u>"

Do you see complacency rearing its head it an area of your life? Has the enemy lulled you into thinking you are okay and there's nothing more to do when God is clearly calling you higher? List that area below.

_____
_____
_____
_____

"*Complacency! Please don't think that remaining in a stagnant complacent place is equivalent to staying steady or holding ground. It's actually moving backwards.*"

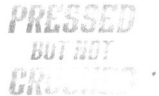

I'm a firm believer that we need to bring things to the light in order to bring about change. The good news is we aren't working in our own strength here. I love that I can bring any issue to God and say, "Please help me fix this." And He jumps right in when I humble myself and surrender it to Him. So we're going to take the area(s) you listed above and we are going to give it God.

Prayer: Father, I repent for being complacent in the area of _____. I surrender this area to you and I say have Your way. Bring conviction if/when I fall into complacency ever again in Jesus' Name. Amen.

Holy Spirit, what are the next steps for me concerning this area? Write them down.

_____
_____
_____
_____
_____

Holy Spirit, show me your strategy for execution. Write it down.

_____
_____
_____
_____
_____

Week 6: Day 5

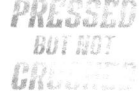

Isolation. Isolation is a trap.

I've seen it many times. People who keep pulling away for long periods of time. The enemy LOVES it. He feeds them lies. There's no one around to rein them in with God's truth and, before you know it, they have gotten themselves bound by something new. A new shackle. New chains. Bound by new ropes that weren't there before.

God values community. Healthy community. I would also submit to you, if every single person in your community agrees with everything you say, get some new recruits. People with fresh eyes. Who haven't drunk the Kool-aid. People who are committed to calling you higher in your destiny, purpose, and calling. Not just lamenting the hard knocks of life with you. Healthy community is key.

What was the most impactful sentence/paragraph from pages 132 – 136? Why?

_____
_____
_____
_____
_____
_____

"There's no such thing as a 'Lone Ranger Christian.' God designed us for relationship."

ACTIVATION

Are you in Isolation? If yes, ask Holy Spirit, "What am I running/hiding from? What lie am I believing about community? What is the truth?"

_____
_____
_____
_____
_____
_____
_____
_____

Let's Review And Celebrate Our Progress Together!

Friends, thank you so much for joining me on this journey! Hearing how many of you encountered Holy Spirit while reading through *Pressed But Not Crushed* made writing this devotional a no-brainer. I pray it helped you encounter your Maker on a deeper level than you ever have before.

In the Introduction to Week 1, I asked you to answer a few questions. Let's revisit them:

1. *"What am I looking to get out of this study?"*

How did you answer this question initially? What do you feel like you actually got out of the study?

_____

_____

_____

_____

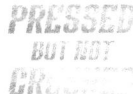

> 2. *"What piece of armor am I most looking forward to discussing and why?"*

How did you answer initially? Did this piece of armor actually turn out to be your favorite? If so why? If not, which one took you by surprise and why?

_____
_____
_____
_____
_____
_____
_____
_____

Now I want you to ask *Holy Spirit* the third question:
> 3. *"Which piece of armor needs to be strengthened the most in my life?"*

_____
_____
_____
_____
_____
_____
_____

How did Holy Spirit use this piece of armor to strengthen you over the last six weeks/30 days?

_____
_____
_____
_____
_____
_____
_____
_____
_____

I am BEYOND proud of each and every one of you. This devotional was designed to be very introspective, but not in the way the world defines introspection. This devotional was designed to set you on a journey of getting comfortable sitting with Holy Spirit and examining your life through His perfect eyes. We did this without condemnation and surrounded by His love and encouragement. Not many people have a strong growth game. Once things get uncomfortable, they run. Once their flaws or areas of opportunity are brought to light, the temptation is to sweep it under the rug. Dealing with the issues can feel daunting.

You proved that you're a fighter and have a strong growth game by completing this process. Now I hope you will continue it. If you're thinking "HOW?", my suggestion would be to get a journal and continue the process of sitting at His feet on a regular basis. Ask Him what He wants to talk about. Ask Him for strategy concerning your life. Ask Him to help you to be transformed into the image of Christ. Grab the declarations that impacted you the most. Make a list of them and put it somewhere very visible. After a while, you'll begin to flow and all these disciplines will become second nature to you. Voila! A relationship is formed, deepened, and strengthened. Praise God!

I want you to know that I would love to hear from you personally. Please stay connected with me on your journey. You can find me on most social media platforms (Facebook, YouTube and Instagram) by searching the name Cassandra Bellevue.

Every now and then I'll feel led by the Holy Spirit to come on social media live with an encouraging message or prophetic word. To be the first to know about livestreams and speaking engagements, please join my email family. You can sign up at CassandraBellevue.com.

Some of you are going to want to go even deeper and I get it. If you're like me, you don't want to miss out on ANYTHING God has for you. I call you the Destiny Chasers. Not because your destiny and purpose are illusive or running away from you, but because you are pursuing all that God has for you with all your soul, mind, and strength. As a Certified Life Coach, I offer individual and group life coaching to help catapult people just like you into their God-designed destiny. Many who come to me feel lost, directionless, stuck, or as if their life has no meaning or purpose. By the time Holy Spirit gets done with them, they have the tools they need to confidently pursue the destiny He's already placed in their DNA!

You can find out more about my life coaching services on my personal website: CassandraBellevue.com.

Final Declaration and Prayer

In closing, I want to leave you with two powerful tools. Here is a dynamic declaration for you to declare over your life, followed by a blessing prayer to seal it all in.

Declare this over your life:

Father God, I plead the blood of Jesus over my life right now in the name of Jesus! Thank you for the equipping that has transpired in my mind and spirit over the last several weeks. Father, I seal in the good work that YOU have started here!

Father, I declare and decree that I will put on the **Belt of Truth** daily! I will gird myself in the truth of who You are and in the truth of who You say that I am. I commit to doing my best to take every thought captive that comes against Your TRUTH, period! Secure me in all knowledge of all Your attributes, Father God! May I come to experience the truth of who You are and never look back. Remind me of who You say that I am, that I may confidently pursue the calling on my life.

Father, I desire to live righteously. I take up my **Breastplate of Righteousness** in this season and every season. I commit to walking in integrity and making the right decisions even when it's unpopular and inconvenient! I will guard my heart against the temptations that will attempt to sear my conscious or harden my heart. Give me an extra measure of Holy Spirit conviction when I need to course correct in my life. I declare and decree my "yes" will mean yes and my "no" will mean no, as I pursue living with integrity.

Father, I take up my **Gospel Shoes, my shoes of peace**. I declare that peace is my portion as I go about Your business today and every day. Fear is not my portion. I rebuke fear and come out of agreement with anything that may suggest that You are not my protector. Show me how to abide in You and exercise my authority to stay in a place of peace.

Father, I raise up my **Shield of Faith** to stop the fiery arrows of the devil! No matter how many promises you have made, God, the answer is YES in Christ and through Him the AMEN is spoken by us to the glory of God! I agree with Your word and I will know Your Word by keeping it ever before me. Your logos word, the prophetic words You've spoken over me through others and in my quiet times with you, God. I say Yes and Amen! I have faith that Your word will not return void!

Father, I put on my **Helmet of Salvation**! The hope of my salvation is secure in You! You want to accomplish something bigger through me than I could ever accomplish on my own. Have Your way in my life. I will not waiver from the truth that my hope is built on nothing less than Jesus' blood and His righteousness!

Father, I finally take up my **Sword of the Spirit**! As the only offensive weapon in this armory, I will never stop wielding your Word in every situation in my life. Your Word is life! Your Word is Power! Your Word is active, living, and breathing. The Word of the Lord will be on my lips in every season, making way for my promised victory. In Jesus' mighty name I pray. Amen!

Now I want to speak a prayer over you before you go.

Father God, bless these faithful ones who have come through this study believing they would encounter You and be forever changed. I declare and decree over each one that the progress they have made over these last 30 days/six weeks is secure and cannot be stolen from them. They will be counted among those who are living victoriously and walking out their purpose.

God, I ask that You help them set their faces as flint. I pray that NOTHING will be able to deter them or distract them from the race set before them. I pray for supernatural healing of minds, hearts, and souls in this season so they can lead others successfully in the future.

Hedge them in by Your Holy Spirit Fire and make their lives' callings and destinies too hot for the enemy to handle! In Jesus' mighty name! Amen!

★★★★★

I cannot fully express the excitement I feel over every one of your lives. There is a race set before each one of you. Some of you are shopping for new shoes. Some of you are heading to the track. Some of you are lacing up your running shoes. Some of you are in the starting blocks waiting for the gun to go off. Some of you are running with all your might, and some of you are so close to finishing well. No matter where you are and what you're doing, do it as unto the Lord. If God is for you, who can be against you?! That means the victory is already yours! If you don't quit, you win.

I can't wait to hear how you are fulfilling your destiny! Don't be shy! Reach out to me on social media or my website (CassandraBellevue.com) so I can celebrate with you.

Please also consider leaving a review on Amazon to testify about what God did in your life during this study! I would be so grateful! Do not underestimate how powerful your testimony is. It will encourage others to challenge themselves to change their lives for the better.

www.ingramcontent.com/pod-product-compliance
Lightning Source LLC
Chambersburg PA
CBHW082211070526
44585CB00020B/2369